Writer Gives Warning On Liberalism, And Discovers Likely Neurotic Symptom Cure

This is a book about my continued warning about liberalism and on what I think political will help save my country (USA), but I am starting this book off with this chapter involving my life long battle with neurotic symptoms. I experience my first neurotic symptom as a small child due to being whipped for wetting the bed.

After reaching adulthood and around the age of twenty-four I suffered another neurotic symptom that robbed me of much of my peace of mind in the company of other people. It isolated me to the point that to experience the most relaxation and peace of mind being mostly a loner became my more suitable option.

Since that time and now at the age of seventy-four two additional neurotic symptoms has been added to the grand total. Still, I adhere to the old saying: "Anything that doesn't kill you will make you stronger in someway". Referring back to when I was around age thirty my world really seemed to be coming apart.

I started having terrible nightmares, I would jump out of bed running full sprint, running from only God knows what. I dreaded the night and having to go to sleep, but I'm a survivor and never lost hope. Then out of the blue in some store I spotted a book title, I can't remember where, all I can remember is it read, "The power of positive thinking by Dr. Norman Vincent Peale".

Just thinking back, now tears begins to flow, Writing through tears that book saved my life and sanity. It said positive thinking can change your behavior; I totally embraced it with nothing to lose. It was so long ago, but I think it gave Philippians 4:13 as a positive thinking bible verse to repeat. I paraphrase the bible verse to repeat as: "I can do all thing through God which strengthens me".

Writer Gives Warning On Liberalism, And Discovers Likely Neurotic Symptom Cure

I would repeat that bible verse over and over to myself at least fifty times and more every day. And the nightmares quickly went away and to this day have never returned. After six months later a change came over me that made me feel that I could do anything I made up mind to do. From that day forward I knew without a doubt that positive thinking could change behavior because it had changed me.

So, soon after which was around 1971 I begin my search for a self-made phrase that would restore my complete relaxation and peace of mind around other people. I would create a phrase and use the positive thinking technique to test it on myself to see if it would help me in some way. I knew that sometimes it could take as long as six months for a positive thinking process to fully kick in.

Over a period of forty-six years I have experienced many false positives all to no avail. But, I may be jumping the gun on my latest created positive thinking quote which I think show the most promise ever, and I have decided to introduce it in this book. I have decided after one week that this positive thinking quote may be a 1000 years mental health breakthrough and if lost may take another 1000 years for it to happen again.

For those that don't know how the positive thinking technique work let me explain: Take any short phrase or quote and repeat it over and over to one's self a minimum of fifty or more times every day. The more times it is repeated the quicker it breaks through to the subconscious mind. Also, to make the positive thinking phrase or quote more potent, add through God, which strengthens me or some other deity at the end of my quote.

Now, here is how I am going to go about this: I am going to hide two positive thinking quotes among the

Writer Gives Warning On Liberalism, And Discovers Likely Neurotic Symptom Cure

words in this book. One is the 1000 years neurotic symptom breakthrough-healing quote. And the other one is to help one feel more secure. Good luck. I can't give a one hundred percent guarantee to anything. But, I believe beyond a shadow of doubt that this positive thinking quote will bring comfort and healing to millions for a certain type of neurotic symptom.
F. L. SIRMANS LOG: 22 APRIL 2017, 2142 HOURS.

I0397095

IS ASTROLOGY BEHIND THIS SINISTER LIBERAL NEWS MEDIA COINED PHRASE, "THE LAST PERSON HE TALKS TO"

In this modern day and time can you believe it? Folks, I'm just a lowly neurotic self-made writer, but I think maybe the sinister liberal news media is using the Zodiac sign of Gemini to try to characterize the president. Why else would they keep saying things like, "The last person he talks to" wins the day. And there is other stuff, but I will leave it at just that. I rest my case.
SIRMANS LOG: 14 APRIL 2017, 1333 HOURS.

THE USA MUST WEAN OFF THE WELFARE STATE TITTY, PERIOD.

I'll repeat it again Sam, in spite of socialism and being a sugar daddy welfare state the USA is still the economic engine of the world economy. But, in this writer's view we as a p.... dependent welfare state has a survival glass jaw.

We the USA as a welfare state has the financial burden of feeding, housing, and caring for nearly half of the nation, where is our staying power to finance a war. We are at the mercy of a pinprick that may collapse the entire economy.

A government in a free nation must never take on a

Writer Gives Warning On Liberalism, And Discovers Likely Neurotic Symptom Cure

financial burden more than supporting a military, administrative cost, interior, and the very few things the people can't do for themselves, period.

Where are the statesmen, Where are the men and women of sound mind and judgment with strong long-term survival instinct's? I have drum beat and pounded and pounded to no end on what must be done, but still no one wants to hear me.

I'm tired, why repeat again anymore what I have already repeated well over 1000 times. Glory be to God. I love my beloved homeland the only home I've ever known. Now, I weep. Hallelujah. Amen. (Click here to understand slave blood killings)
SIRMANS LOG: 05 APRIL 2017, 2154 HOURS.

OFF YOU MARCH MADNESS: JUST A ONE MAN'S PERSONAL OPINION:
I wonder whom the great genius was who decided not to show the score during march madness. If you ask me, which no one has? Well, I'll give my opinion anyway, how can the TV audience build suspense and get emotionally into the game if they don't know what the hell the score is. It had to be a liberal that made that decision in this writer's view. Duh.
SIRMANS LOG: 01 APRIL 2017, 1839 HOURS.

IMMIGRATION AND THE "LITTLE RED HEN" EFFECT: DUH.
With a well-established and embedded welfare state like the USA and Western Europe it is shallow and stupid to think the immigration problem can be solved. Who needs to do hard grinding tough work in blazing heat or freezing cold to survive? Not I said the dog, not I said the cat, and not I said the duck.

Western Civilization never had a dire problem with

immigration, culture rot, or moral decay before minimum wage laws came about. Getting rid of all minimum wage laws entirely is the only thing that can possibly save the USA and Western Civilization, period.

A simple fact in economics is a business can't charge more than the working people can afford to pay and stay in business. That simple fact is what snuffs out inflation and keep prices affordable in a true free market place economy. But, a minimum wage law blocks prices from dropping and that allows for a never-ending inflationary spiral.

The 1938 USA minimum wage law created an "Inflationary monster" that enabled our welfare state to grow to today's super monster size, which has almost destroyed our culture, our moral and family values, and our proper norms and traditions. I beg, Get rid of the minimum wage laws before no means of survival is left.

Starve the "Welfare state beast" that is the only way to destroy it; otherwise it is going to destroy the USA and Western Civilization, period. Then guess what culture will fill the void and inherit the earth?
SIRMANS LOG: 28 MARCH 2017, 1154 HOURS.

GREAT WRITER GOES OFF ON A RANT AND ALMOST LOSES IT!
In terms of USA and western civilization survival, out of control liberalism is the #1 danger and threat. It is far more dangerous than a nuclear weapon threat or anything else in this writer's view. I'm no brilliant great intellect or anything of the sort, in fact I am a slow plodder, but I know my ass from a hole in the ground.

I thought everyone knew that there has never been a society that survived without the strong foundation of the nuclear and extended family system, we seem to be a nation with a death wish. Our nuclear and extended family system is in almost total ruins, our judgment, our common sense, and our weak survival instinct is almost that of a spoiled child in terms of raw survival.

I assure you a nation have nothing in terms of raw survival without a strong nuclear and extended family system, period. And anyone that doesn't know that simple fact is an ignorant fool in term of human survival.

Government as a free social and family provider is a fool's game that may be here today but gone tomorrow. Then, who you gonna call? Government as a free family provider destroys the nuclear and extended family unit, moral and family values, proper norms and traditions, and everything else that holds a society together.

When the nuclear family or anything in nature is not needed for survival it starts ceasing to exist according to nature's supreme law of "Natural selection". A sugar daddy welfare state eliminates the survival need for the traditional nuclear and extended family unit. And that alone sounds the death knell to that society or nation in term of long-term survival.

Where is the USA survival instinct, what is there to live for if not for future generations, self-serving can lead to insanity and self-destruction. God, calm and ease my pain. Amen.
SIRMANS LOG: 22 MARCH 2017, 0104 HOURS.

PS: AND ANOTHER THING:
Western civilization is in a no holds barred culture world war III plus or minus religion, which Western Civilization is going to lose, unless all minimum wage laws are gotten rid of. That is because banning all minimum wage laws is the only things that can get rid

of western Civilization's nursemaid welfare states.
Proper discipline is really the answer to the west's
problem, but a p.... welfare state will never man-up to
proper discipline. Duh.

**IF SET FREE, USA ECONOMY LIKE A PHOENIX
WILL RISE UP AND SAVE OUR BELOVED NATION**
This great writer just decided to go bold and speak
truth to insanity. The republicans control all three
branches of government and have the power to save
the USA and western civilization.

All that is necessary is just repeal the arch-evil 1938
socialist minimum wage law and set the USA economy
free. But, I'm afraid that will never happen because in
my view they lack the foresight or the survival instinct
to see that as the answer.

I know beyond a shadow of a doubt that it is
impossible for a true unrestricted free market place
economy to fail, period. Practically all of the human
survival foundation building blocks in the USA and
Western Europe are in ruins.

Still, like a Phoenix only a true unrestricted free
market place economy can rise up out of almost ashes
and restore our nuclear and extended family units back
to health. And make good character supreme again
along with adequate bartering capacity to withstand
any financial or natural disaster. God, save my beloved
USA. Amen.
SIRMANS LOG: 17 MARCH 2017, 1526 HOURS.

THE OBAMACARE TAR BABY:
The first fact is liberals and liberalism can't save the
USA because that is the very thing that is destroying
the USA in this writer's view. So, that leaves the only
chance of USA freedom and the country ever being

saved up to the republicans.

The old saying: "No guts no glory" is as true today as it ever was. In a weird way Obamacare may be a blessing in disguise in terms of the USA surviving as a free nation or even at all. That is because the Obamacare riddle cannot be solved without a nation saving sacrifice.

In fact the real truth is the USA economy cannot digest Obamacare without totally collapsing, anyway. The only way to solve the Obamacare riddle is what I have been drum beating for well over twenty years. Just simply repeal the arch-evil 1938 socialist minimum wage law and that will set the USA economy truly free to work its magic and save our nation from total doom.

However, folks I am a neurotic self-made crude writer with an opinion, and I believe the liberals will finally get their long desired authoritarian socialist state within five years. God knows, I pray that I'm wrong. **SIRMANS LOG: 14 MARCH 2017, 0131 HOURS.**

THE RUSSIAN PREMISE:
This writer compares all of this hyped Russian emotionalism stuff to the Salem witch-hunt. That is because of an extremely false liberal premise in the first place, it is sheer ignorance, superstition, and emotionalism gone amuck, period. Can the USA survive liberalism gone amuck?

Wow! I am now learning why individual freedom is almost unheard of throughout all of history. Now I know, it is because of liberals and liberalism. Don't get me wrong now, I love liberals and this would be a dark and dreary world without liberals, they are the spice of life.

Writer Gives Warning On Liberalism, And Discovers Likely Neurotic Symptom Cure

In fact liberals were out front in ending slavery and the advancement African Americans has made in the USA today. But, balance in survival is key, and out of control extreme liberalism is what's destroying the USA and Western Civilization, period.

Under control liberals are great, but there is nothing on earth more dangerous than out of control liberals and liberalism, period.

There is nothing innate about being a liberal. Being a liberal is mostly a lack of never having faced survival threats, or not enough discipline or hardship. A welfare state breed's liberalism, never in history has the poor ever been liberal and corrupt until our welfare state came about. Many liberals have become conservative overnight when a mugger slammed one up side the head, or a burglar cleaned out ones home.

I constantly harp on and on about getting rid of our minimum wage law. The reason is only a true free market place economy with no restriction on competition, prices, or wages can provide the discipline to control liberals and liberalism. I harp because I want to keep my individual freedom.

I believe the USA and Western Europe has now arrived at a point where liberalism is now factually out of control. To prevent being totally engulfed there are only two ways to bring liberalism back under control, period.

Those two ways are number one: Get rid of all minimum wage laws and the discipline of a genuine true free market place economy will bring liberalism back under control. Number two: Chaos and disorder will demand authoritarian rule with an "Iron fist". There are no other choices.

SIRMANS LOG: 03 MARCH 2017, 1404 HOURS.

Writer Gives Warning On Liberalism, And Discovers Likely Neurotic Symptom Cure

THE POLITICAL THINKING IN THE GREAT OLD USA TODAY IS FATALLY FLAWED I'M SICK OF IT!
All of this "Holier than thou" stuff, I'm sick and tied of it. It is just another concealed form of hate and contempt. Whoever falls for it and tries to be perfect will self-destruct. People of decency and goodwill will accept one for who and what they are, period. Never let anyone dehumanize you into a perfectionist, to err is human. Can the USA survive liberalism? That is the question that needs to be answered.
SIRMANS LOG: 02 MARCH 2017, 1336 HOURS.

The founding fathers never set the USA up to be an omnipotent cradle to grave caretaker welfare state. All throughout history for over 6,000 years until the "New deal" came along the nuclear and extended family system kept its role as the foundation and backbone for USA human survival.

Because of the welfare state, now our nuclear and extended family system is in almost total ruins with the morning after pill and abortions on demand, same sex marriages; and mass killings in the womb galore, duh. It's no wonder why the USA and Western Europe can't survive without Immigration, sheer insanity.

It is no longer a matter of will it, but when is this minimum wage hogtied phony USA economy going to totally collapses. And leave the USA with no foundation left to rebuild upon.

I so hoped with the republicans winning the "Trifecta" the possibility of this arch-evil 1938 socialist minimum wage law would get repealed. But, now I am afraid the republicans will never see the light and save the nation from this arch-evil law.

Writer Gives Warning On Liberalism, And Discovers Likely Neurotic Symptom Cure

To me it is very simple why I have wrote against this arch-evil law for so long, I just can't see any way to keep the liberals from turning the USA into a failed authoritarian socialist state as long as this evil law exist, period.

Sure, the republicans seemingly has the most power now, but I assure you they will barely put a dent in the tide of liberalism as it march on to a socialist state. If you think I'm wrong, wait until there is any real pain from social program cuts, to boot politically the republicans will be sent packing.

There is only one way to turn the tide and prevent the great USA from becoming an authoritarian socialist state; the republicans must set the hogtied USA economy truly free by repealing the arch-evil 1938 socialist minimum wage law. Just like the democrat's risked going down with the ship by saddling the nation with Obamacare.

Obamacare is tar baby, touch it and you are stuck. The republicans should have stayed away from it and focused on repealing the arch-evil 1938 socialist minimum wage law. Now, the republicans politically own Obamacare and will get blamed for all of its unsolvable problems. And, I won't be one bit surprised if the Dem's get their own "Trifecta" in 2020.

However, in liberal's hands we will become authoritarian almost overnight because of the chaos and lack of order. It is now down to welfare state versus sheer USA survival, we can no longer afford both; things are fast coming to a head.
SIRMANS LOG: 26 FEBRUARY 2017, 1423 HOURS.

LAST CHANCE FOR THE REPUBLICANS TO SAVE THE USA
Again folks, I am just a lowly self-made neurotic writer

with a cause to help save my beloved USA homeland. I pull no punches and call a spade a spade, period.

As to our beloved USA president, I know he means well and has the best of intentions, good luck. But, he is up against a well-established well-embedded all-powerful liberal welfare state. Plus, riding shotgun for the welfare state is a shallow minded hysterical irrational republican hating predominate liberal news media. All of that being said, political speaking there is no painless way to save the USA from liberalism and the dire culture, moral, and economic fix the liberals have put this great nation in.

The only chance this writer see to save the USA from total doom is for the republicans while they have the "Trifecta" is to repeal the "Arch-evil 1938 socialist minimum wage law". And let the chips fall where they may, the sacrifice of saving our freedom and the nation is worth it, period. No sacrifice, no saving individual freedom and the USA, period.

Otherwise, nothing is going to stop the liberals and their created welfare state from achieving their long desired complete authoritarian socialist state, period. God, I ask in your name, save my beloved homeland the great USA.

Again, I have tried to get it through thick sculls that to break the liberalism grip and save the USA, anything less than repealing the arch-evil 1938 socialist minimum wage law is like pissing on a barn fire expecting to put it out, duh.
SIRMANS LOG: 18 FEBRUARY 2017, 1404 HOURS.

A SHALLOW LIBERAL NEWS MEDIA COMES WITH A WELFARE STATE TERRITORY, SO, QUIT YOUR BITCHING AND DEAL WITH THE WELFARE STATE.
Never forget that the overwhelmingly liberal news

media we have today is a micro cosmos of nearly half of the whole USA. A shallow conniving corrupt predominate liberal news media is what the USA is reaping after 80 years plus from our do-for-me welfare state.

What you are seeing from the liberal news media is a snapshot of a nation's culture and morals in almost total ruins. And it is only going to get much, much worse. Only repealing our arch-evil 1938 socialist minimum wage law can wean the USA off the giant welfare state titty, period.

That is the only thing that is going to restore our nuclear and extended family system and save this nation's culture and morals from total doom. God save my great beloved USA.

SIRMANS LOG: 14 FEBRUARY 2017, 0124 HOURS.

PS: FOR ANYONE BESIDES A FLAMING LIBERAL THE LIBERAL NEWS MEDIA IS TRYING TO MAKE IT IMPOSSIBLE FOR HIM/HER TO GOVERN THIS GREAT COUNTRY, THE USA. DUH.

WILL THE USA SURVIVE AS A FREE NATION?
I know I'm wasting my breath, but a wall or nothing else is going to save the USA and Western Europe except one thing. And that one thing is to wean off of their welfare state titty's, period.

How you do that is get rid of all government enforced minimum wage laws, because that is the job and role of the free market place to decide the maximum wage a business can pay and still make a profit. There is no other way; no free nation can survive very long without the discipline of a "No minimum wage true free market place economy", period.

Writer Gives Warning On Liberalism, And Discovers Likely Neurotic Symptom Cure

Here in the USA food is already beginning to rot in the fields, and we all must eat to live. The reason no one will hear me yet, is because the suffering have not become great enough, but that day is closer than we think.

SIRMANS LOG: 12 FEBRUARY 2017, 1025 HOURS.

SPORTS HUMOR:
I can't remember the origin of the myth, but I do remember reading many years ago that a curse was put on the Atlanta Falcons football team.

Its been so long ago that I will just have to paraphrase, I think the writer said that the "First Atlanta Falcons football stadium was built over an old Indian burial ground". And that is the cause of the curse.

I remember well reading that article many years ago. Maybe with the new stadium the curse will be lifted.

SIRMANS LOG: 09 FEBRUARY 2017, 1140 HOURS.

PRESIDENTIAL EXECUTIVE ORDERS:
I'M ONE THAT BELIEVES THAT IT IS ALWAYS BETTER TO BE SAFE THAN SORRY:
SCROLL DOWN FOR LESS THAN 5 PERCENT KNOWS:
Presidential executive orders are basically the same powers any CEO has for managing his/her company. Before the "New deal" and the first 158 years of this nation presidential executive orders

had very little effect on private enterprise or normal civilian life at all.

That is because very few people depended on the government for hardly anything. Now, government is driving the economy and damn near everything else, what a pity.

PS: THE GREAT USA IS GREAT BECAUSE IN THE PAST IT WAS ALWAYS RULED BY LAW, NOT IDEOLOGY, EMOTIONALISM, CONSERVATISM, LIBERALISM ETC. GOD HELP US.

ADD ON #1
The fact is this writer can dissect and understands the inner workings of an economy as well as anyone. I have concluded that the USA culture, morals, and economy all are on a course toward total doom.

It is so frustrating to me that no matter how long I keep drum beating and flailing away sounding the primal alarm stress call that repealing the arch-evil 1938 socialist minimum wage law will reset our course toward that "Shinning city up on the hill".

All the USA need to do is simply repeal the 1938 socialist minimum wage law, the republicans now has the "Trifecta power" that I have long written about, but I'm afraid they totally disagree with getting rid of this arch-evil law. But, I assure you if the republicans don't go for the jugular and repeal this arch-evil law while they have the power, nothing can stop the liberal from making the USA an authoritarian failed socialist state, period.

Writer Gives Warning On Liberalism, And Discovers Likely Neurotic Symptom Cure

However, if the republicans repeal this evil law it will untie our bound USA economy and a genuine true free market place economy will kick in. The untied USA economy will slowly purge and bring into balance the cost of living staple foods and medical prices so they can't get above what the poor can pay out of pocket.

The reason why prices and the cost of living are so out of sight is because government subsiding won't let the prices come down. By government giving money to the poor and needy on an individual basis means the merchant is not forced to keep prices down lower enough for the working poor in order to stay in business.

If government is going to pay the poor on an individual basis it should be done with stamps that can only be spent in a government commissary, clinic, of housing unit only. Otherwise it is impossible for the USA economy to survive much longer.

There is no mystery here, an economy just simply have too many variables, but like mother nature a genuine true free market place without a hog tying minimum wage law will keep everything in balance and save the USA.

However, like nature has a birth and death cycle, an economy has a normal natural boom and bust cycle to get rid of moral decay, culture rot, and anything else that is getting out of balance.
SIRMANS LOG: 31 JANUARY 2017, 1803 HOURS.

LESS THAN 5 PERCENT KNOW PROFIT IS THE LIFE BLOOD OF EVERY FREE NATION, PLUS ULTRA LIBERALS HATE PROFIT:
Knowing something as simple as where do practically all government income and wealth originate from, I doubt more than 5 percent of the U.S. population can give the correct answer. You will get answers like all kinds of taxes, licenses, fees, tariffs, or whatever, which all will be wrong.

Right answer: Practically all of government income and wealth originates from some form of private U.S. business profit, period. It's like a small kid thinking all butter and eggs originates from the grocery store.

Dwindling private U.S. business profit is why the USA is 20,000,000,000,000 in debt; U.S. businesses simply don't generate nearly enough profit to support our ever-growing bloated welfare state, period. And you are going to convince me that the USA economy is not going to soon totally collapse, duh.

Sure, I may be a little bit crazy, but I'm not shallow and stupid.
SIRMANS LOG: 31 JANUARY 2017, 1111 HOURS

NOTE: 30 JANUARY 2017:
I know that most of my writing is in the extreme to 98 percent of the USA population. And many times I have doubts and wonder why the hell I keep writing this stuff. Then, I see all of the ado and uproar over a less than severe temporary change of policy.

Writer Gives Warning On Liberalism, And Discovers Likely Neurotic Symptom Cure

To me that is proof enough that unless our arch-evil 1938 socialist minimum wage law is repealed first, nothing is going to prevent the liberals from making the USA a failed socialist state, and individual freedom be damned. God knows I pray that I'm wrong.

Otherwise, I seriously doubt if the USA can ever be saved from deadly liberalism, there are simply just too many powerful Monday morning quarterbacks.

NOTE: 28 JANUARY 2017:
As a self-made neurotic writer of almost supernatural wisdom I believe after everything is said and done by this new administration, our all powerful liberal welfare state will end up chewing this administration up and spiting it out, period. Only repealing the arch-evil 1938 socialist minimum wage law can save the USA from total doom, period, in this writer's view.

NOTE: 24 JANUARY 2017:
Sure, an authoritarian country can sell natural resources and exploit it's own people and other weaker countries to gain wealth. But, only a free country with a genuine true free market place economy can generate real wealth and be able to feed all of it's people, period.

ONLY REPEALING OUR 1938 SOCIALIST MINIMUM WAGE LAW CAN SAVE THE USA. LETTING CITIES AND STATES SET THEIR OWN MINIMUM WAGE LAWS WOULD PREVENT NATION-WIDE COST OF LIVING INCREASES THAT IMPACT EVERYONE:

Writer Gives Warning On Liberalism, And Discovers Likely Neurotic Symptom Cure

Caution: As a self-made writer I often express some extremely strong views, and I'll just leave it at that. Not a few shallow minded people think I'm a fool and don't know what the hell I be talking about. But, in my view anyone that thinks the USA can keep on borrowing money to pay for an ever-growing bloated welfare state is the real fool.

With over eighty years of mass liberal government dependency buildup there is no painless way out for the USA dire situation. Only returning to a genuine true free market place economy by repealing our 1938 socialist minimum wage law will give the USA a fighting chance of surviving, especially as a free nation.

It's just too late; nothing can stop the U.S. economy from soon totally collapsing. Returning to a genuine true free market place economy will only give the USA a fighting chance of survival instead of regressing all the way back to the Stone Age. God knows, I pray that I'm wrong on this.
SIRMANS LOG: 21 JANUARY 2017, 1418 HOURS.

WRITER BELIEVES USA WELFARE STATE IS GOING TO CHEW TRUMP UP AND SPIT HIM OUT:
Believe it or not, only a genuine true free market place economy nation supplies the discipline to maintain order without using an iron fist. Without a true free market economy 80-100 years is the limit, then only the "Iron fist" can keep the peace. Today the USA is nearing that point; only repealing the arch-evil 1938 socialist minimum wage law can save us.

If not that, at least government must establish or

contract out it's own commissaries, clinics, and housing units. And use stamps, tokens, or scrip for all who qualify and to be used only in government establishments.

Never forget we still live in a well-established welfare state and benefits and social programs is survival to masses of people. Plus, I believe drastic cuts in social programs and benefits will mean mass booting of republicans in 2018, we'll see.

The structural policies I advocated are the only way to escape the grip of our all-powerful welfare state. Otherwise, our great white father welfare state is simply too power and is going to chew Trump up and spit him out, we'll see.

SIRMANS LOG: 19 JANUARY 2017, 1359 HOURS.

THE MYTHS AND IGNORANCE CONCERNING HEALTH INSURANCE

GREAT WRITER FEELS GOVERNMENT SHOULD ESTABLISH OR CONTRACT OUT IT'S OWN COMMISSARIES, CLINICS, AND HOUSING UNITS.

Lets face facts folks, anyone with an ounce of economic knowledge should know that the U.S. economy as is, is going to soon totally collapse. This policy I advocate is guaranteed to save the U.S. economy and restore our culture and morals all in one swoop.

When government aids the poor and needy I advocate protecting the USA free market place economy from involuntarily inflating and driving the cost of living further and further out of sight.

Writer Gives Warning On Liberalism, And Discovers Likely Neurotic Symptom Cure

Also, I advocate the government establish or contract out it's own commissaries, clinics, and housing units. And use only stamps, tokens, or scrip for all who qualify and be limited for use in a government establishment only.

By doing this it will stop the rise of consumer cost of living in its tracks. And it will also reduce and keep the cost of food and medical cost at a level where the working poor can pay out of pocket. The reason that will keep consumer cost of living prices at a level the working poor can pay, is because billion upon billions of government dollars won't be dumped into the U.S. private economy on an individual basis.

Government dumping billions into the U.S. private national economy on an individual basis is what drives the cost of living out of sight. The "Amount" of money the government spends helping the poor and needy doesn't matter, it is the individual basis that drives the cost of living up for everybody.

You simply can't have a genuine true free market place economy with billions of government dollars on an individual basis dumped into the private U.S. economy, period. And to add salt to injury the arch-evil 1938 socialist minimum wage law blocks the U.S. economy's purging power to protect itself and the nations culture and morals.

I know a great many people totally disagrees with almost everything I write, and sometimes my own doubts creeps in, but duty forces me to push doubt aside. Also, I wonder sometimes if it's possible for the USA to be saved as a free nation.

I see the USA culture, morals, and economy approaching total ruins, yet so many see life as business as usual. And the nuclear and extended family unit, which is the foundation for human survival is tossed aside and disregarded like a bad penny. God save my beloved homeland.

Of course I advocate that government establishing it's own commissaries, clinics, and housing units should first test the policy. Start with a city like Detroit, they have a lot of empty building and if successful, then test it on one state, and if still successful go nation wide.
SIRMANS LOG: 12 JANUARY 2017, 1955 HOURS.

CONCERNING HEALTH INSURANCE:
Almost everyone is setting around thinking that Obamacare or any insurance company is the problem with health care. Nothing could be further from the real truth on the matter. Medical insurance in health care is just a facade that hides the true villain, which is "Mr. ultra high cost".

A word to the wise, when the cost of medical care gets above what the poor people's nuclear and extended family system can pay out of pocket, then that is a problem only a true free market place economy can solve, period. Once the evil 1938 socialist minimum wage law is gotten rid of entirely a true free market place economy will bring everything back into balance and save our great USA.

Otherwise, the USA liberal march toward a failed socialist state will continue at warp speed.
SIRMANS LOG: 09 JANUARY 2017, 2214 HOURS.

Writer Gives Warning On Liberalism, And Discovers Likely Neurotic Symptom Cure

WHO KNOWS WHAT TO BELIEVE ANYMORE, IS THERE AN AGENDA?
As a writer of almost supernatural wisdom I will state this as a fact, Mr. Trump and the republicans has one last chance in a lifetime to save the great USA. That last chance is to repeal our liberal enacted arch-evil 1938 socialist minimum wage law. Otherwise, I believe they will fail big time and soon get the boot.

Once the republicans get the boot thereafter the Dem's and liberals will have clear sailing to finish turning the USA into a failed socialist state. It is a fact that only a genuine true free market place economy with its purging power discipline can keep a nation free.

Once the free market place is corrupted or destroyed in a nation it is only a matter of time before only an authoritarian government using an "Iron Fist" can maintain order, period. The evil 1938 socialist minimum wage law neutered and took away the purging power discipline from the USA economy.

That is why this great country is split right down the middle with liberals galore, never in history has the poor ever been liberal and morally corrupted to the core. And they are killing unborn babies in the womb by the millions. God save my beloved homeland.
SIRMANS LOG: 07 JANUARY 2016, 1913 HOURS.

04 JANUARY 2017 JUST OVER A FORTNIGHT AWAY THE "TRUMP" ERA BEGINS
Folks, I am a self-made writer. And I want to

Writer Gives Warning On Liberalism, And Discovers Likely Neurotic Symptom Cure

restate that I know that 99 percent of the American (USA) people disagree with me on getting rid of our 1938 federal minimum wage law entirely. The reason for this wide gulf in belief is a lack of understanding on how a true free market place economy is supposes to work by the general public.

One of the key factors in a free market place economy is "Buying power", But the 99 percent pro-minimum wagers never think about those words in the big picture. Ignoring "Buying power" is why sometimes it can lead to requiring a wheel barrel load of money to buy a loaf of bread.

There is a simple formula when you have a genuine true free market place economy: "You can't get blood out of a turnip", which means no merchant can charge more than the poor can pay and stay in business. That is because there is never enough rich and well to do people to keep an economy afloat.

You see government is not part of the economy, there are only two players in any economy and they are a seller (merchant) and a buyer (consumer). And if there is no thumb on the scale by the government favoring either side they will always balance each other and keep prices affordable for the poor. The problems begin when government won't settle with just collecting taxes and being a neutral referee for both sides.

The shallow minded liberals discovered that under the pretense of caring about the poor they could stay in power by providing all kinds of free goodies. That was the foot in the door, now government is dumping billions upon billions into the private U.S. national economy on an individual basis inflating and driving the cost of living higher and higher.

Without the government dumping all of these billions into the private economy on an individual basis it would be impossible for food prices and hospital bills to get above what the poor could pay.

There is only one way the government can aid the poor and needy and not eventually collapse our U.S. economy: Government must establish or contract out its own commissaries, clinics, and housing units and use separate token or scrip for all who qualify. That way all of the billions won't be getting into the national economy on an individual basis contaminating and driving the cost of living out of sight.

The amount of government spending is not the problem, it is the "Individual basis" spending dumped into the private national economy that does the damage. Mr. Trump has saved the Supreme Court, and as for as I'm concerned that was a Godsend.

Never forget, we live in a well-established liberal welfare state, and liberals dominate education, the news media, and the minds of our young, which is our future. So, I can't see Mr. Trump and the republicans prevailing in the long run unless the 1938 socialist minimum wage law is repealed and the government stops dumping on an individual basis billions of dollars into our national economy.

Like the Dem's at all cost they rammed Obama care down the nation's throat, now while the republicans have the chance they had better at all cost do what they must to save this great nation. This nation is culturally and morally bankrupted to the core and teetering on a total financial collapse. And the Dem's and liberals has no clue. Lord have mercy on this nation's sole.

The Dem's and liberals are like zombies program to tax, tax, tax, and spend, spend, spend as if ignorance is bliss. Still, I love um; we are all Americans (USA) and our brothers' keepers. **SIRMANS LOG: 04 JANUARY 2017, 1530 HOURS.**

SURE, AN EPIC DEATH BATTLE TO SAVE WESTERN CIVILIZATION IS GOING DOWN. BUT, THE BATTLE IS NOT WHAT ALMOST EVERYONE THANKS IT IS. THE REAL BATTLE IS CONSERVATISM VERSUS LIBERALISM AND IGNORANCE, WITH LIBERALISM ALREADY HAVING TAKEN OVER DAMN NEAR EVERYTHING.

LIBERALISM AND IGNORANCE IS THE TRUE IDEOLOGY THAT HAS AND WILL FINISH DESTROYING WESTERN CIVILIZATION UNLESS DRASTIC ACTION IS TAKEN SOON.

ONLY BANNING ALL MINIMUM WAGE LAWS CAN SAVE WESTERN CIVILIZATION BEFORE IT COMPLETELY SELF-DESTRUCTS DUE TO LIBERALISM AND IGNORANCE. SURE, ALL OF THIS OTHER STUFF MATTERS BUT FIRST THINGS FIRST.

ABORTION: THE RICH HAS ALWAYS MURDERED FUTURE UNBORN BABIES IN THE WOMB, BUT NEVER HAS THE POOR MASS MURDERED IN THE WOMB UNTIL AFTER OUR

"NEW DEAL" WELFARE STATE. IT IS A CRIME AGAINST NATURE NO MATTER HOW ONE LOOKS AT IT.

ANYONE THAT KNOWINGLY AND INTENTIONALLY MURDERS FUTURE UNBORN BABIES IN THE WOMB PAYS WITH OVER POWERING GUILT, OR DEVELOPS CONTEMPT FOR HUMAN LIFE ITSELF TO AVOID GOING INSANE. (ISMDH).

CAN THE REPUBLICAN ESTABLISHMENT STOP THE "DONALD" BEFORE HE CROSSES THE 2016 PRESIDENTIAL FINISHING LINE?
It is my experience with family members and those with severe flaws; they can force one into making a deep hard emotional choice that may defy reason. With some people you have to either love them or leave them there is no shallow middle ground. I believe that is the case with Mr. Trump's supporters, they have made their love choice. Still, it is the issues that nurture this love.

Almost everyone knows love can be blind. Many parents have learned the hard way it is not wise to put down an undesirable suitor. Mr. Trump's supporters know who he is and are not looking for a Mr. perfect. They made their choice and who is to say they are wrong, I can't, only God knows. Just like in a marriage, the ones almost everyone predicts will fail, often don't, and vice-versa.

No matter what anyone may think Mr. Trump has a great issue focused formula for winning. But, I feel there is a diplomatic character element that makes the formula seems more of a vice than a virtue to the majority.

Take away the stinging insults, the cold harsh put

downs, and the eye for eye that leaves everyone blind, and then you have a pure non-stoppable winner in my view. There is no doubt he has the issues the Republican Party has totally ignored.

There is no secret here, anyone could take these same issues and get the same results Mr. Trump is getting, but a cold harsh voice of authority is a must or you won't be believed or trusted.

However, I may be totally wrong on this whole matter, Mr. Trump may still rule the roost, who really knows? "No chain is stronger than its weakest link".

Free speech and the truth shall set you free. But, liberalism and ignorance doesn't want to hear the truth unless it agrees with it. The first and second amendments to the US. Constitution must prevail at all cost, lets don't get it twisted, y'all.

I thank God for any man/woman that won't lie down and rollover, and is willing to stand up for all of our first amendment rights. Praise be to God.

It is now the welfare state or we; so, starving the welfare beast out of existence is the only way of getting back to sanity before we all are over-run and praying five times a day.

Anyone that thinks that the USA or any welfare state can be saved without first getting rid of its minimum wage law is a fool in my view. Sure, I may be the one that is really the fool, but I'm sure history will prove me right on this.

I wrote on my website FLSirmans.com a while back that Mr. Trump was just the catalyst before the main event that is going to save this great country.

Writer Gives Warning On Liberalism, And Discovers Likely Neurotic Symptom Cure

As a super great writer of almost supernatural wisdom I still stand by my first observation. However, only God knows how or when the main event will take the stage. Who knows?

Right now currency-wise all of the USA survival eggs are in one basket, which is a sad dangerous situation. The value of the coin portion of the USA currency must be return back to being within itself, such as real gold, real silver, real copper, or some other precious medal, period.

Otherwise, when this world economy soon collapses the USA will be back to trade and bartering to survive, but with very, very few small farmers and home gardeners almost no one will have anything to eat or barter with, dooms day will be upon us.

No western civilization problems such as immigration, crime, morals, economics etc. today will ever be controlled without first getting rid of all minimum wage laws. The reason is simple: The core or main problem with the west today is self-destruction; it lacks self-societal discipline, due to the minimum wage laws.

In a free society only the economy can maintain proper societal discipline in the long run contrary to the law as almost everyone thinks. Plus, minimum wage laws chokes off the purging power of a true free market place economy and leaves it with no power to maintain societal discipline.

Today, with hardly any societal discipline left there is very little means of stopping liberalism and ignorance from bringing on our total self-destruction. Far too many people today believe survival is owed to them and it is always someone

else's fault if they fail. Liberalism and ignorance
has no true concept of what it takes for this great
USA nation to survive, financial or otherwise,
period.
SIRMANS LOG: 08 MARCH 2016, 2018 HOURS.

**WHY SOME PEOPLE SEEM TO BE LOVED AND
ACCEPTED NO MATTER WHAT THEY DO OR
SAY**   There is an old axiom that has befuddled
reasonable men and women forever. It is the
saying that "To those whom much is given, much is
expected". Hell, I feel it may even be a law of
nature.

I believe people tend to love and accept you the
way you truly are to yourself. And if you are truly a
talented and responsible person that is the way
people expect you to act. I think that is why
liberals can get away with far more than a no
nonsense responsible conservative can, the
expectation is not the same.

I think that is why anyone with great and proper
character that goes down and wallow in the gutter
is not living up to his/her expectation, period, and
will be treated accordingly. It may not be fair but
that is just the way it is.

Some people the more they act up and act a fool
are written off with low expectation and just loved
anyway in spite of their behavior. We all have at
least one those in the family. My grand mother
used to always say, "It takes all kind to make up a
world".

In many families one or two people always
complain, why am I always expected to carry more

than my share of the load. Tough titty, that is just the way it is. Never forget, nature is all about maintaining a balance in the universe.

When you see an extreme it is only creating a counterbalance against another extreme somewhere. Remember what Nixon said about one of his tough guys, sure, he is a S.O.B. but he is our S.O.B.

SIRMANS LOG: 05 MARCH 2016, 1045 HOURS.

A QUICK WORLD ECONOMY FACT:
No matter what the world economic condition may seem, the USA is still by far the economic engine for the world. The big Dragons, the little Dragons, and all others would in no time be in the poor house if the USA economy heart skips a few beats. There is no other market that even comes close to the size of the USA market.

SIRMANS LOG: 12 MARCH 2016, 1614 HOURS.

USA LEADERS FIDDLE WHILE ROME BURNS.
KNOWLEDGE IS POWER BABY
As a writer of almost supernatural wisdom I offer a USA survival blueprint why not follow it. If a better one exists, please disregard. Sure, You can laugh, but history will be the final judge. You have been enlightened, you know the one and only thing that must be done, now get it done.

Me, this little lone neurotic writer attacking this big giant liberalism Ogre is like David attacking Goliath. Don't look a gift horse in the mouth.

NOTICE:

Writer Gives Warning On Liberalism, And Discovers Likely Neurotic Symptom Cure

I will almost always say bridle liberalism. The reason is liberalism is not necessarily a bad thing in fact liberalism makes a more caring and better world, but it will also destroy everything if not disciplined and kept under control. Either an iron fist literally type government or a government with a true free market place economy can keep liberalism bridled.

Since 1938 the USA no longer has a true free market place economy due to the government enforced minimum wage law. And without a true free market place economy the USA has no way to maintain societal discipline thereby allowing liberalism to take down this great nation.

These do-good make everything right liberals are on a warpath about gun control, they can barely sit still and are wiggling in their seats. What they don't understand and are too shallow to realize is out of control liberalism is the cause of the gun problem in the first place.

However, I'm one that believes liberals forcing threatening gun control down the nations throat is the one thing that will definitely give republicans a Trifecta or complete a Hat Trick in 2016.

If you want a better society you first must have a better class of people, period. From lack of societal discipline this USA nation is being over run with moral decay and culture rot, that is where the real problem lies. Almost all of this nations old tried and true norms and traditions have been corrupted by liberalism.

They have been replaced by new insane anti-survival norms like same sex marriages and mass killing of future unborn babies in the womb. I won't preach, I will end by saying you have been enlightened on what must be done to save the USA from total doom.

Gun violence is one of the least of this nation's problems, our way of life and survival itself is on a slow countdown. And here we are fiddling while Rome burns.

As a writer of almost supernatural wisdom I have said a thousand times the one sure thing that will save the USA from total doom, so there is no excuse why this great nation should go the way of the great Auk (Click on >) Auk.

No matter which way the wind blows, I'm here to warn you that only a genuine true free market economy with no kind of government wage or price control can provide the discipline to save the USA and western civilization, period.

You see, only an economy without any kind of government wage or price control will have the necessary purging power not only to discipline and protect itself, but will also protect the nation's culture, moral, and spiritual values from over powering rot and decay like what is eating us alive today.

Repeal the insane arch-evil 1938 socialist minimum law now. Let the only thing that can possibly save the USA and western civilization, which is a genuine true free market place economy with no choking government wage or price controls, what so ever work its miracle.

Agree or not, like it or not, without a doubt I am right on this, I will bet the farm on it. There are certain things about human nature that never changes, things such as spite, envy, jealousy, hate, superstition, and the rest of our emotions. Things of this sort haven't changed one iota in over 2000 years.

Concerning societal discipline: As late as the nineteen fifties or sixties many small towns and rural areas in the USA didn't even bother to lock their doors. So, concerning societal discipline what has changed in today's world, the key word is discipline. The USA has practical no societal discipline left today.

That is the main reason we have so many nuts committing mass killings with guns today. It takes discipline to isolate or weed out those that won't conform. Sport teams use tryouts to see who conforms and the military uses basic training to see who conforms. Well, a healthy society on a much larger scale must have some means to isolate those unwilling to conform.

I believe those that has the mentality to go out in a blaze of hate and terror will always show some tell tale signs well in advance, its just that those that knows are not telling or speaking up. Many first grade school teachers to a high degree can point out even then the ones most likely to be in trouble with the law eighteen years later.

I will bet my bottom dollar that at least one person knew everyone of these mass killers was a danger to society in some way before they acted. The reason the USA doesn't have the societal discipline to isolate and deal with these type of individuals is because of our minimum wage law. Don't roll your eyes and laugh, because I know you think that is stupid and doesn't make sense.

Writer Gives Warning On Liberalism, And Discovers Likely Neurotic Symptom Cure

Let me explain, the shallow minded see the minimum wage law only in terms of how much more money one is paid on a job and they can't get pass that. Sure, only a fool wouldn't like to make a living wage or make more money. And getting any kind of a private sector pay raise is a good thing and will work. But, on a large or national scale with everyone getting a forced government raise it may give everyone more money, but more purchasing power will be just an illusion.

It is an illusion because every forced government wage increase results in a higher cost of living increase. And over time the cost of living increases will far out distance any salary increases. The minimum wage law is why twenty years ago ones salary versus cost-of-living would buy far more in the grocery store then than it will today. And if moral decay and culture rot doesn't doom the USA first consumer cost of living soon will.

Buying power is what truly and really counts, not more and more lesser and lesser-valued inflated dollars, which the shallow minded and less informed can't seem to comprehend.

Yet, if the government raised the minimum wage ten dollars it would kill off most small businesses and consumer-cost-of-living would really sky rocket even more. Anyone that know the basics of true economics should know that any kind of government wage or price control doesn't work in the long run and will rip apart a nation's culture and moral inner fabric.

The real danger and destruction from any kind of government imposed wage or price control is what it does to the entire USA economy. Any kind of government imposed wage or price control de-nuts and renders a free market place economy practically helpless with almost no purging power left. Purging power is what gives an economy the discipline to protect itself, the nations culture, moral, and spiritual values.

Starting in 1938 the USA economy's hands has been tied behind its back due to the enacting of our minimum wage law, and ever since then the USA as a nation has been without societal discipline leaving the nation almost without a rudder.

Another big problem with the USA economy is the USA government is trying to manage and control it. That in itself is an impossible task simply because there is just too many variables. The government shouldn't be forcing a minimum wage on the private sector and it shouldn't be in the stock market either.

Plus, the biggest no, no of all is for government to ever become a social and family provider. Once that happens there is no peaceful way out for government, because when money starts running out the mobs is going to be coming after politicians with pitchforks. Only repealing the insane arch-evil 1938 socialist minimum wage law can prevent this from happening, otherwise there is not enough societal discipline left to keep western civilization from regressing all the way back to the stone age.

Government should run the country, the military and stick to collecting taxes and get the hell out of the way to allow a genuine true free market place economy to prevail. Government should stay with what it does best collecting taxes, running the country, the military, and leave the economy to the private sector, period.

Writer Gives Warning On Liberalism, And Discovers Likely Neurotic Symptom Cure

Plus, that was mainly the way it was before government decided to take over private enterprise by not allowing the private sector to set its own wages and prices (The insane arch-evil 1938 socialist minimum wage law ended private control of the USA economy). And until control of the USA economy is back in the hands of the private sector it is impossible for this nation to survive, period.

As a writer with awesome creative thinking ability along with almost supernatural wisdom I believe even if the republicans do complete a hat trick in 2016 liberalism will still rule the day. In the USA and other welfare states around the world liberalism is on autopilot.

Which means the only thing that can bridle liberalism enough to save western civilization from total doom is a true genuine free market place economy, period. I can avoid direct eye contact with anything I want to. But, here is the catch; it is impossible to have a true genuine free market place economy with any kind of government enforced wage or price control in effect, period.

So, even if the republicans do get a Trifecta in 2016 by gaining control of both houses of congress and the presidency it won't save the USA from total doom, unless the arch-evil 1938 socialist minimum wage law is repealed once and for all.

The only true benefit I can see for a minimum wage law in the first place was to inflate our currency to finance and keep our liberal created welfare state in power. Without a minimum wage law a pure free market place economy will purge out inflation. Now, to change gears, just like the life and death cycle is necessary for life to exist, the boom and bust cycle in an economy is

necessary for an economy to exist. It is a law of
nature.

The USA economy is going to collapse that is a
given, no one knows when, but a big bust cycle is
long overdue. My grave concern is what is going to
happen afterward. I'm not out to scare anyone
one, I'm just a lone writer with a one man's
opinion, and hopefully I'm wrong.

It is just simply impossible for any society to get
through a long overdue bust cycle without a strong
nuclear and extended family system in place, which
the USA no longer has.

Repealing the arch-evil 1938 socialist minimum
wage law will restore our strong nuclear and
extended family system along with strong morals
and spirituals values providing time don't run out
on us. Otherwise I can't see any way around total
doom, period. You can call me crazy, a nut, or
whatever, but that is the way I see it, sorry.

Before 1938 a lone woman with a purse could walk
through a black neighborhood or any neighborhood
at midnight and no one would harm her. Today
what has changed, the come about of the insane
arch-evil 1938 socialist minimum wage law put a
stop to societal discipline. And since that day our
once real true free market place economy lacks the
purging power to stop inflation, culture rot, or
moral decay.

Lets face it, liberalism and its created welfare state
has destroyed individual responsibility and
accountability to the point that the USA may no
longer have the capacity to remain a free people.
In spite of out of control liberalism and its created
welfare state we in the USA still has the most

individual freedom found anywhere in the world.

Only the second amendment is keeping us free, but history is not on us gun owner's side. The insane arch-evil 1938 socialist minimum wage law must be repealed now, not tomorrow. Otherwise, one way or another big stud liberalism is going to eventually have its way with the 2nd amendment in my view.

NOTE:
The worst mistake any conservative with strong great character can commit is try to win the approval of liberalism, because if they can make you a perfectionist then you destroy yourself by dehumanizing yourself.

People don't love you because you are perfect; people love you because you are human. Never constantly deny any negative, make one statement per negative, then repeat that has been addressed and move on, period.

Remember, rightly or wrongly no one likes a whiner. Let them take a hike if they can't take a joke.
SIRMANS LOG: 06 NOVEMBER 2015, 0018 HOURS.

GREAT WISDOM:
Lately I'm hearing a constant drum beat from conservatives and republicans on cutting taxes to save the USA from doom. Sorry, it is too late for that liberalism is much too embedded and powerful and will come roaring back with a vengeance if this

path continues.

I agree under normal circumstance that should be the normal thing to do, but the masses upon masses of government dependents at the first sign of real pain politically is going to send conservatives and republicans packing.

The better and only way, again I repeat if conservatives and republicans have any chance of saving the USA from doom they must repeal the insane arch-evil 1938 socialist minimum wage law, then a true genuine free market place economy will kick in and do whatever it takes to save this great nation.

It is a one shot chance, if it is not taken or misses the mark, shallow minded liberalism will once and for all drive the final nail into our coffin, this I guarantee.

Only a true free market place economy has the power to bridle liberalism enough to have a fighting chance of saving the USA from total doom, period. **SIRMANS LOG: 29 OCTOBER 2015, 1754 HOURS.**

BRIEF FOOD FOR THOUGHT ADD ON:
Sure, the rich and powerful has always aborted and killed babies in and out of the womb. But, as to the rest of society mass killing of future unborn babies in the womb is a modern thing within the last fifty years no matter the reason.

Nothing has advanced civilization more than conquering armies and in the distance past mass raping almost always was seen as just part of the reward bounty. Hell, even in slavery if every life that resulted from rape were aborted there would be a lot fewer blacks around today.

Yet, some blacks are setting on their high horses demanding that every life resulting from a rape be killed in the womb. Studies have shown that the trauma of being a raped victim in many cases is eased by the love from the innocent child. I'm not condoning anything, I'm just saying...
SIRMANS LOG: 27 OCTOBER 2015, 1938 HOURS.

THE POWER OF FORGIVENESS:
What my harshest critics will never understand is no one acquires almost supernatural wisdom without enduring unusual great suffering to survive in some way, period. I feel if I weren't spiritual to the core I would have long fallen by the way side.

It is virtually impossible to mentally destroy anyone that can genuine love and forgive. I just repeat to myself as much as necessary, I can wish all people goodwill through God who strengthens me.

THE ARCH-EVIL DESTRUCTIVE POWER OF A MINIMUM WAGE LAW
If I had to choose just one thing that has all but totally destroyed western civilization and will soon finish it off: That one thing is a government forced minimum wage law on private enterprise.

Without a government forced minimum wage law consumer inflation cannot exist to propel a welfare state. It is the welfare state that has produced all of these masses upon masses of dense shallow minded liberal thinkers with no true concept of moral or economic survival, period.

Sure, they think I'm a fool, a hater, or some kind of monster that don't know what the hell I'm talking about. But, I know I'm right on this and we'll all soon find out when this phony USA economy totally collapses and send us all back to the Stone age.

SIRMANS LOG: 25 NOVEMBER 2015, 1122 HOURS.

FREE ADVICE ADD ON:
No one asked my advice, but I decided to give a little free advice anyway. There are two main ways to control or motivate people; it is through love or fear. I am as self-defending as anyone. Some believe love is best but fear is more dependable.

At least in the old days the west had sense enough to prop up strongmen and that kept order, but somehow along the way liberalism creep made that a no, no. Now, almost total disorder abounds, because the west to this day still believes one size fits all.

In many cases involving an army or fighting force it must boil down to option odds, meaning ones chances of surviving is equal or greater staying and fighting than running away. Strongmen shoot deserters on sight.

SIRMANS LOG: 15 NOVEMBER 2015, 0855 HOURS.

WORDS OF GREAT WISDOM:
What I keep trying to get through thick sculls is we must bring back a genuine true free market place economy, then the phony climate change liberalism cause, the debt problem, the immigration problem, the health care problem, the crime problem, and

every other grave problem we have will solve itself.

Only a true free market place economy has the
power to keep liberalism at bay, anything less is
like pissing on a barn fire expecting to put it out.
These politicians will be making promises until
doomsday, yet higher taxes and more debt grows
daily.
**SIRMANS LOG: 09 NOVEMBER 2015, 1300
HOURS.**

FOOTBALL PLAYERS DEMAND:
The purpose for going to school is supposes to be
to get an education, period. How long can the USA
remain a free people, duh? This is just another sad
escalation of liberalism flexing its muscles; get use
to it, much more to come.

With a problem of this sort in the final analysis it all
boils down to a lack of societal discipline in some
way. But, what can you expect, unless our insane
arch-evil 1938 socialist minimum wage law is
repealed it is impossible for the USA to be saved.
We are now entering the early stage where only an
iron fist literally can maintain order.

You can't keep individual freedom without self-
responsibility, self-accountability, and self-
restraint, period. Soon the people will demand that
government take away our individual freedoms just
to maintain order. Just keep living, you'll see.
Liberalism is out of control and deadly.

There is no doubt in my mind that out of control
liberalism is going to take the great USA down
unless we get back to a genuine true free market
place economy and soon. I wish I could break my
pen and walk away from this, but it is a calling and
I just can't.

Writer Gives Warning On Liberalism, And Discovers Likely Neurotic Symptom Cure

SIRMANS LOG: 08 NOVEMBER 2015, 0045 HOURS.

BRIEF INSERT:
Like the gospel without exception I'm one that totally believes in the strong nuclear and extended family system and the free enterprise system. That gives over 6000 years of proven tried and true survival experience backing up my writing. So, how can I be a wrongheaded fool and nut case? Duh?

Welfare states and governments always fail or go broke sooner or later, only the nuclear and extended family system and the free enterprise system have withstood the test of time. The USA nuclear and extended family system is almost totally destroyed because there must be a survival "need" for anything in nature to exist.

The USA government as a social and family provider welfare state has almost completely eliminated the survival need for a nuclear and extended family system, a system that has assured the survival of the human species for over 6000 years. My God! What a price the USA is gonna pay for this severe lack of wisdom. I am talking about the very foundation for human survival itself.

This could mean back to the Stone Age or even human extinction. With the awesome almost supernatural wisdom I have it is a burden to be one of the very few that can see what's coming our way. No one else has to believe anything I write. However, I don't write just to impress anyone, I only write what I truly believe.

Writer Gives Warning On Liberalism, And Discovers Likely Neurotic Symptom Cure

NOTE:
There is no such thing as a free market place economy with any kind of government enforced wage or price controls, period. However, in the private sector unions should have the power to drive wages as high as they can, but government should stay with collecting taxes and let the free market place police itself.
SIRMANS LOG: 23 DECEMBER 2015, 2050 HOURS.

TRILLION $ USA SPENDING PACKAGE
For the wrong reason in my view the republican establishment is doing the right thing when caving just to hold on to power thereby waiting for a one-punch liberalism knockout. All most of these modern day shallow minded conservatives that can't see the big picture know is to cut here or cut there, which is political suicide when millions upon millions is solely dependent on government for their survival.

Thank God they haven't got their way because the resulting economic pain would definitely have put liberals back in total power and all would be lost maybe forever. As it is the republicans stand a better than fifty fifty chance of getting that one punch liberalism knockout opportunity with a trifecta after November 2016.

Only a one-punch knockout blow can bring liberalism under control enough to save the USA and western civilization from total doom. Need I say more, by now most people already know what my "said" one punch liberalism knockout is? Hint: 1938, Thank God.

Writer Gives Warning On Liberalism, And Discovers Likely Neurotic Symptom Cure

I assure you our USA welfare state economy is going to soon totally collapse, it is impossible for it not to. Only by repealing our arch-evil 1938 socialist minimum wage law first can total anarchy back to the stone age be prevented, period.
SIRMANS LOG: 17 DECEMBER 2015, 1650 HOURS.

GREAT WRITER, FREDDIE L. SIRMANS SR. GOES OUT ON A LIMB ADDRESSING TERRORISM HOPING IT WON'T BE SAWED OFF.
The west is in a quandary and can't understand why it is so hated and unappreciated instead of loved by some cultures and religions. It is morals and family, fool! Hell, who with even a feeble survival instinct and any sense of true decency not be against out of control liberalism.

If western government forced minimum wage laws on private enterprise is not soon repealed the west will be overrun morally-wise while standing around hugging their pets. The quickest way to destroy any society is for government to do for the people that will weaken their survival instinct by leaving little or no survival challenge to face.

Liberalism and the welfare state for the most part has destroyed the strong survival instinct and common sense in the USA and only getting rid of the minimum wage laws can untie our economy to save us.

The young and unborn is 100 percent of our future that is why strong culture and morality is a must for future survival. Whereas, liberalism tends to live only for self in the now, me first, I want mine, I want it all, and that scares the hell out of certain cultures and religions.

Writer Gives Warning On Liberalism, And Discovers Likely Neurotic Symptom Cure

There is nothing on earth more threatening to future survival than out of control liberalism, period. With the mass use of the "Morning after pill", the mass killing of future unborn babies in the womb, and same sex marriages, how can there be a long-term future for western civilization?

Already Western Europe and Japan can't repopulate themselves. Plus, I didn't mention the vast amount of men into porn and all of the women with hidden toys, (Prostitution article). Wake up and get a grip America, western civilization is slipping away, fools.

That should scare the hell out of anyone with a strong normal healthy "Survival instinct". Out of control liberalism will surely bury us all unless wise men and women repeal our insane arch-evil 1938 socialist minimum wage law, period.
SIRMANS LOG: 03 DECEMBER 2015, 1600 HOURS.

GREAT WRITER'S VIEW ON THE USA GUN PROBLEM AND MODERN ECONOMIC THINKING:
Guns have been plentiful in the land of the USA ever since Plymouth Rock (1620). But, never since has there been a problem with guns until after 1938 for a very simple reason. The reason is norms and morals are what determine a nations character.

1938 is when liberalism got its grip on this nations throat with the enacting of the insane arch-evil 1938 socialist minimum wage law. Ever since that day liberalism and the welfare state has gone about

destroying the USA nuclear and extended family system and all good moral and spiritual values in my view.

Writer Gives Warning On Liberalism, And Discovers Likely Neurotic Symptom Cure

That has left the USA today as mostly a nation of shallow naive government dependents that see government as some kind of omnipotent sow with nipples that can be sucked on forever.

I pity the fool that thinks the USA economy ship is unsinkable and can take on just one more free load to no end.

Wisdom, wisdom, wisdom, the dumb and stupid thing about depending on a government and welfare state for survival is it destroys the nuclear and extended family system.

There have never been and never will be a society that survived without a strong nuclear and extended family system. In terms of human survival the nuclear and extended family system is everything, and when you destroy that neither the government nor anything else can survive for very long, period.

Repealing the insane arch-evil 1938 socialist minimum wage law will begin restoring the USA only savior the all-powerful "Nuclear and extended family unit". It is not a matter of the USA economy collapsing; it is a matter of how soon.

I've said this before, now I will say it again. Only a genuine true free marketplace economy has the power to save the USA and Western Europe. However, the key is it is impossible to have a genuine true free marketplace economy with any kind of government "Forced" price or wage control law in effect.

There is no greater survival guarantee on earth than a genuine true free marketplace, period.
The biggest mistake in modern economic thinking is the belief that government can manage and control an

economy successful over time.

Government managing an economy over time is an impossible task because there are just too many variables. If government would just keep hands off a true free marketplace economy would manage and control itself. A genuine true free marketplace has no favorites and the powers that be always hate that.

Before 1938 government stayed mostly with just collecting taxes and running the country. And let the private sector set its own prices and wages the way it was ever since the founding of the country.

Basically ever since 1938 liberalism and a welfare state mentality has been running the USA economy. And it is impossible for this great nation to ever be saved unless the private sector gets back to setting its own prices and wages, period.

I am a man of almost supernatural wisdom and can be wrong on many things, but not on the "Must" for the private sector being free to set its own prices and wages if the USA economy is to survival long term, or at all.

The "Key" to long term economic survival is the response to market forces, a private sector genuine true free market place does that well, government never responds to market forces. That is why unless drastic basic structure changes are made soon it will be impossible for the USA economy to survive very much longer, period. And you can take that to the bank.

Unless a basic structure change like the private sector being free to set its own prices and wages again the USA will soon unravel morally, spiritual, as well as financially.

Writer Gives Warning On Liberalism, And Discovers Likely Neurotic Symptom Cure

SIRMANS LOG: 05 JANUARY 2016, 1908 HOURS.

WHAT IS A PRESIDENTIAL EXECUTIVE ORDER?
One of the biggest misunderstood things in the USA today is a <u>presidential executive order</u>. A presidential executive order is suppose to be basically the same as any CEO or company leader issuing an order to his/her supervisors, managers, and employees.

Before 1938 a presidential executive order had almost no effect on the private sector because very few people depended on government for anything. Today government is so big with so many agencies that the private sector is almost totally ruled by government.

President <u>Richard Milhouse Nixon</u> is the one that kicked in the door to the imperial presidency, now, our imperial presidency is a well-established fact.
SIRMANS LOG: 03 JANUARY 2016, 1214 HOURS.

CURRENT EVENT PASSING THOUGHT?
The predominant shallow minded liberal news media allowed Trump to dominate the news as long as he went mostly after republicans. Now, here comes this down in the gutter Cosby soap opera thing? Come on now? Give me a break, y'all.
SIRMANS LOG: 30 DECEMBER 2015, 1636 HOURS.

**WRITER'S BELIEF:
I BELIEVE FORGIVENESS ADVANCES CIVILIZATION AND UN-FORGIVENESS REGRESSES CIVILIZATION. I BELIEVE WITHOUT THE CHRISTIAN RELIGION CIVILIZATION WOULD STILL BE BACK IN THE DARK AGES. THE TRUTH SHALL SET YOU FREE. SIRMANS LOG:**

Writer Gives Warning On Liberalism, And Discovers Likely Neurotic Symptom Cure

31 JANUARY 2016, 0059 HOURS.

WHAT IS A LIBERAL OR PROGRESSIVE?

A jurist once said something to this effect, I can't tell you what obscenity is but I know it when I see it. A lot of liberals are claiming that many of our founding fathers were liberals, I say hogwash. Well, I know this, before 1938 and our welfare state about the only place you could find a true liberal was in a rich family or maybe on a college campus for a very simple reason.

Just facing the elements and the day-to-day struggle to stay warm and keep food on the table made just about everyone a conservative or you wouldn't survive. There was no social or welfare state support system. And it was almost unheard of for a poor black woman to kill a future unborn baby in the womb.

Now, today the poor has the worst morals and are killing more babies in the womb than any other demographic group, all because no one is instilling proper norms and traditions in their young. So, how do you like me now?

SIRMANS LOG: 27 JANUARY 2016, 1615 HOURS.

ESTABLISHED FACTS ADD ON:

Other than an authoritarian type government system, it is impossible to keep a disciplined orderly society without a strong nuclear and extended family system and a genuine true free market place economy. Only adhering to the above said facts can our liberalism swamp be drained to saved the USA from total doom?

Politically it really doesn't matter what party wins what or which individual wins, the USA is past the point of no return toward total doom. And all is lost unless our vast liberalism swamp can be drained, period. The only thing that can save us, hint (1938).

Everything about nature either cycles or ebbs and flows. That is why a genuine true free market place economy will automatically protect itself and a nation through good and bad times. However, liberalism put a stop to that by enacting the insane arch-evil 1938 socialism minimum wage law to buy votes. And until that catastrophic mistake is rectified it is impossible for the USA economy to recover or survive, period.

Sure, the establishment has failed us big time, but what is far worse is to go chasing after falling stars at the end of a rainbow, which I believe is happening. I say go, follow your star, I hope you find your pot of gold. I wish you only the best and hope your future will be bright. As for me: I will continue to count my blessings and keep the faith, praise be to God.

"There is a sucker born everyday. Everything that glitters is not gold. Those that live on hope die fasting. The show must go on. The way to hell is paved with good intentions. The meek not the weak shall inherit the earth (paraphrased).

The Lord works in mysterious ways. We now have millions gullible enough to sell the Brooklyn Bridge to, y'all".
SIRMANS LOG: 22 JANUARY 2016, 1342 HOURS.

PASSING THOUGHT ADD ON:
I don't want to be too clear on this, but, going after the general could be a signal that justice may go hard in a parallel direction soon in my view???
SIRMANS LOG: 20 JANUARY 2016, 1253 HOURS.

TRUMP VERSUS CLINTON:
There is an old saying be careful what you hope and
pray for because you just might get it. I believe the
Democratic Party establishment and liberal news media
have in the past and still do believe Senator Clinton
can take Trump in a general election. In other words,
said parties are hoping and praying these two will be in
the final face off showdown.
SIRMANS LOG: 16 JANUARY 2016, 1244 HOURS.

THE END

FREDDIE L SIRMANS, SR.

WEBSITE: www.flsirmans.com